DIY Simple Inve

A Guide to Simple and Effective Low Cost Investing

by John Edwards

A simple and, I hope, straight forward guide to help ordinary people better understand investments and develop a strategy based on low-cost passive index tracker funds to provide solid long term returns from the stockmarket.

-----for Juno, Eddie, Stan, Alex and Felix-----

Updated Copyright © 2019 John Edwards

Disclaimer

I do not provide personal investment advice and I am not a qualified investment adviser. I am an amateur investor. All information found here, including any ideas, opinions, views, forecasts, suggestions, or investment selection, expressed or implied herein, are **for informational or educational purposes only and should not be construed as personal investment advice**. While the information provided is believed to be accurate, it may include errors or inaccuracies. Because I am writing for a large audience, I can make no guarantees whatsoever that the information contained in this book will be applicable to your individual situation. I encourage you to do your own research before making any financial decision, and to seek out professional advice from an suitably qualified investment adviser if you are unsure.

Contents

1. Foreword by Lars Kroijer - Author of 'Investing Demystified'

2. Introduction
2.1 The Problem
2.2 Who This Book Is For
2.3 Why DIY?
2.4 Why Investing?

3. Living Within Your Means
3.1 Reduce Consumption
3.2 Easy Access Cash Reserve
3.3 The Earlier You Start…

4. Keep It Simple
4.1 Strategy Planning

5. Access to the Markets
5.1 The Markets
5.2 Common Ways to Invest
5.2.1 Unit Trusts & OEICs
5.2.2 Investment Trusts
5.2.3 Exchange Traded Funds
5.2.4 Individual Shares
5.2.5 Passive Index Tracker
5.3 How Safe Is My Money?

6. Market Returns & Volatility
6.1 Equities
6.2 Bonds
6.3 Returns from Equities, Bonds & Cash

6.4 The Right Temperament
6.5 Market Volatility
6.6 Beware Constant Monitoring

7. A Diverse Portfolio
7.1 Asset Allocation
7.2 Risk Profile
7.3 Rebalancing & Mean Reversion
7.4 Climate Change

8. Keep Costs to a Minimum
8.1 Fund Charges
8.2 Broker Platform Charges
8.3 Cost of Holding Low Cost Trackers
8.4 Tax Efficient Investing
8.5 Taxation of Savings and Dividends

9. Active -v- Passive
9.1 The Research
9.2 Vanguard Study
9.3 The Star Manager

10. The Humble Index Tracker
10.1 What Are They?
10.2 How Do They Track the Index?
10.3 Structure
10.4 Who Provides Them?

11. The Simple All-in-One Options
11.1 The One Stop Options
11.2 A Life Time Solution
11.3 The Early Years
11.4 The Later Years
11.5 Options for Taking Income

12. To Conclude

1. Foreword by Lars Kroijer

In an era where abundant information is readily available via the web on a 24/7 basis it is easy for the individual investor to feel overwhelmed and unsure of who and what to trust. Many tell you how to get rich quick, or share pictures of themselves in front of a big house and fancy car, with the implicit message of "just do what I do, or tell you to do".

It is no wonder that many savers are left daunted and confused, and revert to investing their money like they always have, or perhaps follow the advice of someone from their local financial institution and invest in one of their well-known branded products.

John Edwards' "DIY Simple Investing" can help you take back control of your finances, and with it the insight and confidence to withstand all the bombardment of advice and tips. Most often you don't need expensive professional input, and you can do most of the personal finances yourself, better and cheaper, with the help of this book. The answer inevitably includes index tracking investing, and while they are better known than a decade ago, far too many investors are still not fully aware of the tremendous benefits they can offer.

Generally speaking, far too few people have an incentive to tell you about the potentially simple and cheap way you can manage your finances yourself – certainly not people from the financial sector or media who make money from regular investors in a multitude of ways – but "DIY Simple Investing" is an oasis of a sensible approach, and I highly recommend you study the author's perspectives closely.

If you take nothing away from this book other than the merits of index tracking investments – and there are many other great things to take away – then that alone would make the book well worth reading.

Lars Kroijer

Lars is a former hedge fund manager and author of "Money Mavericks - Confessions of a Hedge Fund Manager" and "Investing Demystified - How to Invest without Speculation and Sleepless Nights".

He is also the founder of AlliedCrowds.com - the leading directory and aggregator of alternative capital into many of the world's poorest countries.

2. Introduction

There can be little doubt than many ordinary people struggle to deal with issues of personal finance and particularly such matters as pensions and equity investments. On the few occasions I discuss these issues with friends and relations it seems the subject matter quickly moves on to less challenging topics. However, just because personal finance is not widely discussed or understood, does not mean it is not important.

The Problem

In 2014, the Open University Business School asked a cross section of the population to answer questions currently on the financial education syllabus. They were shocked by the results. Over two-thirds of UK adults answered personal finance school exam questions incorrectly.

Consumers admitted that their current lack of financial knowledge was stopping them from making informed decisions around mortgages (44%) and pensions (43%) right down to everyday products such as ISAs (32%).

The research also suggested ignorance really isn't bliss, with 60% of the 25 to 34 age group admitting that their personal finances give them stress, anxiety and sleepless nights.

A recent report suggested 1 in 10 of us cannot identify the balance on a bank statement whilst 25% of people say they would rather live for today than plan for tomorrow. More than 16 million people in the UK have savings of less than £100, a study by the Money Advice Service (MAS) has found.

According to the latest government statistics, whilst around half the UK population hold a cash ISA, only around 1 in 7 have some form of investment or stocks & shares ISA. I imagine most of these will be an investment taken out with the advice of an IFA or other financial institution. I suspect around 1% or maybe 2% of the population manage their own investments.

These problems are not confined to the UK. A global study on financial literacy carried out by the OECD in 2016 involving 51,000 people from 30 countries found that only 56% of those surveyed achieved a satisfactory score and 40% of the people had not saved in the previous 12 months.

The study confirms that people with low levels of financial literacy are likely to borrow more on credit, and pay off the minimum each month. They are far less likely to save let alone invest for the long term and will have little or no pension provision.

In 2018, personal consumer credit lending passed £215 billion in the UK. According to data from The Money Charity, over 250 people are declared insolvent or bankrupt every day and 1,750 County Court Judgments (CCJs) are issued every day.

http://themoneycharity.org.uk/money-statistics/

Who This Guide is For

The main purpose of this short book is to help those people who want to take more control over their finances and who have a desire to learn and understand what can be widely perceived as a risky, mysterious and complex world.

Making a start to save money, create a monthly budget let alone think about pensions or invest on the stockmarket can be a daunting prospect for those thinking about it for the first time. However, like most things in life, the hardest part is deciding to do something about the situation. To quote a famous Chinese saying 'The journey of a thousand miles starts with the first step'. Once you take the time to read around the subject and break it down into 'bite-sized' chunks, most people of average intelligence will, I hope, understand the basics much better.

This book is written mainly for the benefit of those with little or no previous experience of managing their own finances. I have deliberately tried to keep things jargon-free and use everyday language to keep the subject matter as simple as possible. I hope it will encourage people to take charge of their personal finances and avoid some of the common pitfalls along the way.

I realise that these sorts of books tend to be quite lengthy which, in itself can be off-putting so I have attempted to keep the book as short as possible whilst at the same time, covering some of the more, what I consider to be, essential aspects in a little more detail.

Although I have previously written and self-published 3 other books, they all assume a certain degree of financial knowledge on the part of the reader. This latest book is aimed at the complete novice and I have attempted to address the subject working on the assumption that the reader will have little or no prior knowledge of financial investments.

I also post regular articles on my blog - **diy investor (uk).** For those who may wish to look at some aspects of investing in more detail, there are some 400 articles posted since I started the blog in 2013 which cover many areas of my personal journey so far. The most popular tabs are 'portfolio', 'basics' and 'popular posts' but probably the most relevant section relating to this book would be '**trackers**'.

This book was in part inspired by a development in my personal investment strategy in more recent years which has made me re-evaluate some of my earlier thinking. managing finances is never a finished process and I continue to learn from the many contributors to the comments section of my blog articles and also from reading the variety of practical investment strategies adopted by the wider community of personal finance authors and bloggers.

In this updated 2019 edition of the book I have included a short section on the big issue of climate change which is likely to pose a threat to the global markets in the future. I am hopeful the global community can find some sustainable solutions which can keep the warming within manageable levels but as I have been making some adjustments to my personal strategy recently (see blog), I think potential investors need to be aware of the longer term risks when making plans for the future.

In this book, I will look at all the elements of developing a simple all-in-one diy strategy which I firmly believe, over the longer periods, has every chance of providing a return which keeps ahead of inflation and is much better than the low cash deposit returns we have endured since 2009. In the process individuals who choose to go down the diy route, could save possibly thousands of £s on advice fees.

In the final analysis, I believe for most would-be investors, the most effective investment strategy will be one that is most easily understood by the average person.

It may take one or two repeat readings of some sections before you begin to grasp the concept or method and translate this to your own situation. Be patient, re-read sections you may not take in first time round, persevere and gradually things should become clearer.

Why DIY?

Well, for a start, individual investors now have much greater options on how and where to invest than ever before. The crucial driving force behind this has been the internet and the emergence of execution-only online brokers over the past 20 years or so. These mean that investors no longer need to call a stockbroker or use their bank in order to buy and sell investments. Instead they can access a wealth of information, view charts and performance tables and compare products available at the click of a mouse and do all this for a fraction of the cost.

The rise of the DIY investing platform allows investors to access a wide range of investments from the comfort of their personal computer, smartphone or tablet. A big source of confusion however is the sheer volume of funds to choose from - currently over 4,000 - so any strategy which help to narrow down the options can only be welcome.

I would not recommend a diy approach for open-heart surgery however, for those with average intelligence, the right temperament and a desire to learn, diy investing is very doable. Yes, it's a marathon not a sprint so you will need to be patient; yes, the markets can be volatile so you need to think hard about your temperament, attitude to risk and asset allocation from the outset and yes, some aspects can be complex but your approach is entirely your choice which can be very simple - if you do not understand it, don't do it!

Secondly, the average person will have modest monthly savings or perhaps a small inheritance or pension lump sum to invest. As a result of changes in 2014 to the way advisers are regulated, fewer and fewer people have access to affordable financial advice, at a time when more and more people need it.

The introduction of the Retail Distribution Review in 2014 resulted in fewer, better qualified advisers. They are likely to be targeting wealthier clients who can more easily afford the up-front fees. These initial advice fees typically range from £750 +vat to £3,000 +vat depending on the degree of complexity and the investment amounts involved. There is often an annual review which will involve further fees - typically £500 + vat or 0.5% of the sum invested.

According to a report (March 2016) by the Financial Conduct Authority (FCA), two-thirds of retail financial products are currently purchased without advice, while many people with less than £100,000 to invest are going it alone when choosing pensions, investments and retirement income products.

Those with more modest savings of a few thousand pounds will be increasingly left to fend for themselves and this could possibly mean a choice between DIY or nothing. There is therefore the potential to save a great deal of money by taking a little time to understand the basics and considering the option of pursuing a simple diy approach.

Finally, it must be accepted that however carefully finance and investments are explained, for some it will remain a challenge. For whatever reason - mental block, lack of confidence or just 'too risky and not for me' - I accept that diy investing is not for everyone. I do however think that many, many more ordinary people could learn to take more responsibility for their future financial security.

Why Investing?

We live in a free country - we can choose to save what we earn or equally choose to spend it. For those who manage to live within their means and choose to save, they can put it in a cash ISA or deposit account with a bank or building society - they may even stash it under the mattress. There is no law which says the money has to be invested - so why bother?

I invest my money for several reasons. The main reason is that, over the longer term of 10 or 20 years, it offers the potential to give me a much better return than leaving money on deposit in the building society. For the past decade I have hardly been able to keep pace with inflation on my cash savings however, over the same period, the returns from my investments have averaged 8% each year from a balanced mix of assets. With this rate of growth, a sum of £1,000 invested in 2010 would become £2,000 by 2019. The same sum in a savings account paying interest of 2% would become £2,000 in 2046.

Since 2009, the interest rates on cash deposits have been very low - sometimes under 1% per year. If the return on cash is low, its value or buying power can be eroded over time by inflation. Cash is traditionally regarded as a 'no-risk' option but over a long time horizon - say 25 years - inflation can seriously damage your wealth.

Investments in such things as equities offer one of the best ways to maintain and grow the real value of your money over these longer periods.

Warning It is not advisable to invest on the markets for periods of less than 5 years due to the higher probability of losing capital during a downturn.

My aim in writing this short guide is to try to make the basics of investing as widely accessible to as many people as possible.

Most people are, in part, put off investing by its perceived risk and complexity - however, like most things, once this shroud of mystery is removed and the process is stripped back to the essentials, I think more and more ordinary people will have the confidence to explore the subject in a little more depth and discover some options which may previously have been more obscure.

Others find a simple approach too boring and seek a more 'sophisticated' strategy. What I believe they fail to realise is that unlike other aspects of life where the more effort you put in, the more you get out - with investing, the opposite applies and more often than not the less you do, the better your outcome.

The reader should have a good indication when reaching the end of the book whether they understand the basics of investing a little more - I hope many will, I also accept some will not.

3. Living Within Your Means

It may appear a little strange to start off a book about investing talking about debt. The reality is that for many people borrowing has become a fact of life and therefore must be addressed in the context of personal finance issues. Debt and consumer credit has become a cultural norm in our modern society.

Many people reading this book will be looking towards longer term goals - maybe an investment to help children with university fees or perhaps a more comfortable retirement for example. To make such plans work, you need to save a significant portion of income every month to have enough money left over after everyday expenses to put away in savings or to invest long-term to fund these goals.

It is a fact of life these days that many people have some form of debt - student loans - currently averaging £45,000, credit/store card, possibly pay-day loans etc. Whilst people are paying high levels of interest on these debts, it may be very difficult or impossible to save money. The interest rates on the debt are likely to be far in excess of the returns you may make from investments so it makes no sense to start investing money whilst debts remain outstanding. Certainly I would never advocate using borrowed money to invest on the markets.

It may sound obvious, but the first step to financial freedom is to try to avoid debt in the first place. I know this is easier said than done in the current climate.

For those with some form of debt, make a plan to get out of debt, cut up the credit and/or store cards and try to make do without the 'extras' until the debt is clear.

Reduce Consumption

To get out of debt and move towards saving or investing, most people will understand it would help to increase income. This may not always be possible so if not, it will always be worthwhile to see whether economies can be achieved by reducing consumption. You are not going to make much progress if the money going in at one end (income) is leaking out faster at the other end (spending).

Do I really need this?

Do I really want this?

Can I manage without this?

These are three important questions to ask yourself in relation to most buying decisions. Some things are necessary, essential and desirable - a lot of things are optional - latest gadget, fashion accessory, change of car, expensive holiday etc.

The aim will be to live within your means. If you are, you will have something over most months, and this will be more by planning than luck!

Cultivating this sort of attitude leads to a situation where, instead of you working for money, money will eventually be working for you.

Easy Access Cash Reserve

Before you can consider other aspects of managing your finances, you will need to create a reserve of 'rainy day' money. This will be a sum equal to approximately 6 months essential expenditure to cover e.g. food, rent/mortgage, motor expenses, insurances etc.

This money needs to be put in an easy access savings account. It is there for the unexpected things that crop up when you least expect - illness, redundancy etc. and will provide a breathing space to sort things out and give a little peace of mind and the reassurance of knowing you have something to fall back on.

Once the rainy day money is secured, think about setting some goals to give more focus to the savings project. Children's education, house deposit, holidays, early retirement are some ideas but the list is endless. Once you have your goals in place, work out how much of your monthly income is to be saved - it could be a set amount, £50 p.m. or a percentage of your monthly income 10%, 20%. Make the amount realistic and affordable.

You may find it helpful to keep a check of monthly income and expenses on a spreadsheet or simple pen and paper. Once the figures are broken down into different categories, it may be easier to see where savings might be made. Some common categories would include:

weekly food, gas & electric, council tax, phone/TV and broadband, insurances, work expenses, car costs, entertainment etc. etc.

Be sure to review your savings and goals on a regular basis, say every 12 months to make sure you are still on track.

Also, be aware that during periods of lower interest rates, the value of savings will be gradually eroded if the return on your savings is lower than the rate of inflation. Therefore, cash savings are not totally immune from risk.

The Earlier You Start...

One more point, its never too late to start saving (or investing). Obviously, the sooner you start the better but we are all living longer, so even in your 40s or 50s it's still possible you will have another 40 or 50 years ahead of you.

I will come back to the phases of investing in a later chapter. For now I will just point out that, due to the magic of compound returns, those people who save or invest for 40 years can expect not double the return of those investing for 20 yrs but over **4 times more.**

Later in this book, I will cover some aspects of investing - asset allocation, diverse global investments, bonds and equities. The are all designed to give you a better chance of a decent return on your investment however, **never lose sight of the fact that the easiest way to grow your wealth is to save more money**.

So, whether you are saving in a pension or investing via a stocks & shares ISA, Lifetime ISA or saving in a cash ISA, the principle is the same - the sooner you can start, the more time your money will have to compound and grow.

Some free resources...

For help and advice I recommend 'Debt-Free Wannabe' discussion boards on the MoneySavingExpert.com forum.

http://forums.moneysavingexpert.com

There is Step Change (formerly Consumer Credit Counselling Service), a free charity dedicated to helping people to find a practical solution to debt and money management problems. Advice is available online with their Debt Remedy tool.
http://m.stepchange.org/

The Citizens Advice service provides free, independent, confidential and impartial advice to everyone on their rights and responsibilities.

Finally Advice UK, the largest support network for free, independent advice centres. They operate in some of the poorest parts of the UK, helping people to solve legal and social welfare problems
http://www.adviceuk.org.uk/money-debt-advice/

4. Keep It Simple

"Truth is ever to be found in the simplicity, and not in the multiplicity and confusion of things" Isaac Newton .

Lets be honest, most ordinary people lead busy enough lives without having to think about stocks and shares, pensions and ISAs. For all but a few, these things are about as much fun as a visit to the dentist.

You can make investing as complex as you wish - research individual shares, delve into annual reports, analyse various approaches to asset allocation etc. For those with a real passion for this area of finance and the time to devote to it, there will be some value in the activity itself - maybe as a sort of hobby with the added advantage that it may well provide a positive return.

Bear in mind there are well over 4,000 managed funds to choose from in the UK and a further 400+ investment trusts listed on the FTSE. There are sites such as Trustnet which provide tables showing which funds have performed better over the past 1yr, 3 yrs or 5 yrs but past performance is no guarantee of future performance. For the novice investor, it can be a minefield weighing up the best option to select.

However, for the vast majority of ordinary people, who simply do not have the knowledge, time or inclination to do this, all they really want or need is a simple, low cost plan which makes sense and which they can implement with a minimum of fuss.

The purpose of this book is to demonstrate that such a simple all-in-one, low cost strategy could be a realistic option for any would-be investors and can provide a decent return with a minimum of effort. I say a minimum of effort because the process will require SOME input and a little work on the part of the would-be investor. This book is not intended as a definitive solution and cannot address all circumstances. It is intended as a guide or starting point and I hope it will encourage the reader to explore possibilities of becoming more financially savvy.

For the best chance of a satisfactory outcome, it will be important to start out with a clear idea of

what you want to achieve, and

how you intend to go about it.

This will involve some sort of strategic plan.

Strategy Plan

Planning does not need to be complicated - its really a process of crystallising your thoughts into a coherent document which will make sense to you and which you can refer to over time as a point of reference.

Each plan will be slightly different as it reflects the goals and objectives of the individual. It would include such things as -

* Time frame - how long do you intend to invest your money - 10 years, 20 years, longer?

* Main goals or objectives - more comfortable retirement, children's university education etc.

* Asset Allocation and your attitude to risk and market volatility - equities to bonds mix? Property, commodities?

* Route to achieve your objectives - type of investments, low-cost platform, broker etc.

* Periodic reviews and rebalance (latter will not be needed with Vanguard LifeStrategy funds)

When you have addressed all the angles, you should have a clearer idea of what you wish to achieve and how you are going to get there. Spending a little time on this before you start may prevent expensive mistakes later.

Investing can be as simple or as complex as you wish to make it. The essence of a DIY strategy is that you take control and at the same time, take responsibility for the future rather than leaving it in the lap of the Gods. Therefore the plan or strategy you decide upon is entirely up to you.

I firmly believe that most investors have the ability to achieve long term success by sticking to a simple, no-frills strategy. Such a strategy will be easy to understand, easy to set up and involve a minimum of ongoing maintenance. It will make use of low cost, well diversified investments which correspond to your individual tolerance to market volatility. **It should not involve anything which is beyond your comprehension**.

From time to time, review your plans and strategy to ensure you are still on track. As you gain more experience and confidence, it may be appropriate to revise your initial plans so maintain some degree of flexibility.

The industry is very innovative and there may be new products coming onto the market such as lower cost funds or brokers which may be more appropriate to your needs.

"Everything should be made as simple as possible - but not simpler" Albert Einstein

5. Access to the Financial Markets

So, any debt situation has been addressed, you have your rainy day cash reserve on deposit and you've decided you want to put in place a strategy for the opportunity of a better long-term return.

It may be helpful to provide a brief introduction to the stock market and how most investors gain access to it. Also, the important aspect of investor protection.

The Markets

In the UK, shares are bought and sold via the London Stock Exchange. The main market is the FTSE and this is sub-divided into the largest companies' shares called the FTSE 100, followed by the next tier of medium sized companies, FTSE 250 and then smaller companies found in the Small Cap index. Not all companies in the UK are listed on the stock exchange. Privately owned firms and co-operatives like John Lewis for example are not listed companies.

There are many ways to invest on the market. There is no completely right or wrong way - all the following have some advantages and some disadvantages.

When I started investing, I used a mixture of investment trusts and individual shares - in the early days, my investment returns were hit and miss and lacked consistency. As I have become more experienced and more widely read on this area of personal finance, I think I have had more success…or maybe I just had a bit more luck!

Today, my individual shares have been replaced as my strategy is more developing in favour of passive index funds.

I update my investments on a regular basis and post these via my blog, **diy investor (uk).**

Some common ways to invest are :

Unit Trusts and Open Ended Investment Companies (OEICs) - often referred to as funds,

Investment Trusts (ITs),

ETFs (Exchange Traded Funds),

Direct Shares e.g. Vodafone, Unilever, BT etc., and

Index Trackers

Lets take a brief look at these in a little more detail.

Unit Trusts & OEICs

These are a form of pooled or collective investments usually run by a fund manager. The manager buys shares or other financial securities in many different companies and the investor buys 'units' in the fund. There are literally thousands to choose from . These are by far the most popular method for the average small investor to access the stockmarket.

They are heavily promoted in the financial media and are popular with investors however, charges tend to be a little on the high side for my liking, typically around 0.75% but up to 2% for more exotic sectors. Prior to a ban on payment of commission in 2014 as part of the FCAs Retail Distribution Review, typical charges would have been a lot higher - around 1.7% for the average fund.

Funds are traded just once per day so you will not know exactly the amount you have acquired and at what price until a couple of days later.

Because of the wide choice of different funds - over 4,000, each of which may have different classes and each with a different charging structure, it can be very confusing for the average would-be investor to select a suitable fund.

Investment Trusts

These are a little similar to unit trusts. They are a form of collective investment but ITs are a company in their own right. So, like shares in companies such as Tesco or BT, the shares of trusts are listed on the market and you can therefore buy and sell shares in the investment trust company.

Trusts use borrowed money, called gearing, to try to improve returns for investors. These can work well when markets are rising but also have the potential to increase losses when the markets are falling.

ITs have the advantage of being able to withhold some excess dividend income in good years and pay them out in poorer years, thereby smoothing the income payouts. Some of the more consistent trusts e.g. City of London, have a record of paying steadily increasing dividends for over 50 years. They can therefore be particularly attractive to those investors looking for a steady income from their investments. I hold several ITs in my own income portfolio.

The ongoing costs will vary, but typical charges will range between 0.50% and 1.25% for many of the more popular investment trusts.

Exchange Traded Funds (ETFs)

ETFs are a cheap way of tracking an index e.g. FTSE 100 or S&P 500 (United States). Unlike actively managed OEICs and ITs, they do not have a fund manager who will pick and choose which shares to hold, rather they merely hold all the shares in a particular index.

Charges are typically around 0.40% or less so they can be a very cost effective way of investing. Some brokers place a cap on their platform charges for holding ETFs (and ITs). This often contrasts with funds where a typical charge of around 0.30% often applies and is often capped at a higher level.

Individual Shares

Shares in blue chip FTSE 100 companies are commonly held by some individual private investors - Unilever, Marks & Spencer, Prudential Insurance, Shell Oil, Vodafone and BT etc. are well known and widely held shares.

For a long term 'buy and hold' investor, shares can be an extremely economical method of investing. There are no more ongoing costs as you have with funds and Investment Trusts.

The drawback I find with individual shares is firstly the amount of work needed to carry out thorough research prior to purchase, and secondly their share price volatility. For these two reasons, they may be a less attractive option for those readers who wish to keep it simple!

Passive Index Tracker

An increasingly popular alternative to managed funds, trusts and individual shares are the low cost index tracker funds or ETFs. The costs are very low, typically 0.40% p.a. or less. Some of the trackers have charges of less than 0.10% p.a. - that works out at under £1.00 per year for every £1,000 invested - incredible value for money.

Supporters of passive trackers point out that very few actively managed funds consistently beat the index year in year out, so why pay the extra fees when you can buy a very low cost index fund?

Some individual investors have a portfolio entirely made up of various trackers covering different markets. Personally, I think they have a great deal to commend them and in recent years I have moved some of my personal portfolio into index funds.

Trackers come in two main forms, index tracker <u>funds</u> (either unit trust or OEICs) and index focussed <u>ETFs</u>. Much more on trackers later in the book.

How Safe is My Money?

The financial services industry is closely regulated in the UK to protect consumers. All investment providers as well as brokers need to be registered by the Financial Conduct Authority (FCA).

The rules do not permit brokers to use clients money for their own purposes. All clients investments are ring-fenced, strictly segregated and held in trust. If, by any chance a broker was to go to the wall, their creditors cannot touch your investments or any cash in your account.

As an additional safety measure, the Financial Services Compensation Scheme (FSCS) provides all investors with protection for any default to the tune of £50,000 (increased to £85,000 from April 2019). Therefore, if you are ultra cautious and your total investments exceed this amount, you could spread your investments between 2 or more brokers.

6. Market Returns & Volatility

In simple terms, whereas savings in a bank or building society are all about cash, investing on the markets is mainly about equities and bonds - a quick explanation of both :

Equities

Equities, or stocks & shares, provide investors with the benefits of a part ownership of a company listed on the stockmarket. When you purchase a share in any company e.g. Vodafone or Marks & Spencer for example, you acquire the right to share in the future financial performance and prosperity of the company.

The principal reason for listing on the markets is to raise capital to expand the business. A company does this by issuing shares. Those shares are then bought and sold on the markets. Just like any other type of market place, the price of the shares will rise and fall according to supply and demand, news, trading results, market sentiment etc.

The stockmarket is basically the product of a capitalist system. It enables the business owner to raise capital in return for a share of the future profits in the business. Therefore the business owner(s) does not need to risk his/her own savings or borrow money secured on his own house. Capital is valued more than labour under the system and those who have the drive and innovation and set up thier own business usually make much more money than the employees of the business.

Investors can become a part owner in some of the largest global companies such as Apple, Facebook and Amazon for example simply by buying into a global index fund or ETF.

It's certainly far easier than starting your own start-up business from scratch.

Stockmarkets all around the world are intimately connected and tend to rise and fall together. The largest market is by far the New York Stock Exchange in the USA with around 50% by value of all global stocks. The UK market by contrast accounts for less than 10% of the total market.

Equities offer the prospect of growth derived from a rising share price together with regular payments of dividends. Where the dividend income is not immediately required it can be reinvested to turbo-charge investment returns in the future.

As we have seen, investing in equities will be more volatile than bonds and investing in just one or two individual shares is likely to be extremely risky. Investing in a collective fund holding many different shares will obviously help to reduce this risk/volatility - volatility can be reduced further by investing in the global equity market rather than just the UK market.

Equities can be considered as the driving force of a portfolio - the engine, and have historically provided the better growth and returns over the longer periods.

Bonds

When governments or large companies wish to raise finance, one option is to issue a bond. Government bonds are called 'gilts', with individual companies they are called corporate bonds. Gilts are generally regarded as a safer investment than corporate bonds as they are guaranteed by the government whereas bonds are only as safe as the company that issues them.

When issued, bonds are normally for a fixed length of time. Usually they pay a fixed amount of return every six months, but you can get index-linked bonds which pay a fixed percentage above the rate of inflation.

Investment returns on bonds can appear attractive, however over time just like cash deposits, the value of their fixed returns will be diminished by inflation (apart from index-linked bonds) and this is an important difference to investing in equities where growth of the company which may include dividend income, will generally rise with, or ahead of, inflation. Therefore over the long term of 10 or more years, equities will generally outperform gilts and bonds.

Bonds are usually not as volatile as shares and can add stability to a portfolio over the long term as well as generating a useful income where required. The interest on gilts and corporate bonds is paid gross, and if held within an isa or pension, there is no tax to pay.

Time Horizon

The first rule of investing for me, and I'm sure many other small investors, is **time frame** - the longer you have to invest, the better chances you have of riding out the long term cycles and ups and downs of the markets. You need to allow many years to have the best chance of getting a decent return - therefore it almost goes without saying, to be successful, you should be the sort of person who is able to demonstrate a degree of patience.

If you may need your spare money for other purposes in the next 5 years - new car, holidays, new kitchen etc., then investing on the markets, however tempting, is probably best avoided. Put your spare cash in a bank or building society savings deposit account.

If you are thinking longer term - minimum 5+ years and preferably 10+ years - your investments will have a much <u>better chance</u> of providing better returns than your average cash deposit savings account.

I underline 'better chance' because it is important to understand that investing is all about probabilities and not guarantees.

The Right Temperament

If we accept that investing is a long term project, it follows that you will need a degree of patience to get the best outcome, You will also need to accept that markets will fluctuate - especially equities, so you will need to possess a certain temperament which is closely aligned to the degree of risk you are willing to undertake.

There is a widely held perception that investing on the stock market is very risky. I often read comments in the popular press money pages which suggest it is akin to gambling at the casino where the odds are heavily stacked in favour of the house.

Many new investors are sucked in to making easy money when there has been a prolonged bull market, as we have experienced in recent years. At the start of 2018 markets were at an all-time high with the Dow Jones over 25,000 and the FTSE 100 over 7,700. However, by the end of the year, the Dow was down 2,000 points and the FTSE had retreated below 7,000.

What goes up will eventually turn down but many new investors pile in at the top and are totally unprepared for a 20% loss when the bull run ends and fear grips the market.

"We have seen much more money made and kept by 'ordinary people' who were temperamentally well suited for the investment process than by those who lacked this quality, even though they had an extensive knowledge of finance, accounting, and stock market lore" Warren Buffett.

We therefore need a plan which takes into account our personal capacity and reaction to loss and then put in place a realistic allocation of assets to closely match the degree of risk and volatility we are prepared to take. This is one of the **most important aspects** for the DIY investor to take on board. Some people are natural risk takers and may be temperamentally well suited to a higher exposure to equities, whilst others are naturally cautious and require a more balanced allocation which may include a higher percentage of bonds.

An assessment of our emotional make-up does not need to be complicated. Most people will know whether they are naturally cautious/reserved or carefree/outgoing. Some people are natural risk-takers, others prefer the slow & steady option.

Knowing these basic types will help to select the most appropriate asset allocation.

Of course, for the new investor, it may be the markets are rising fairly steadily for the first year or two with little volatility. The best time to assess whether you have selected the most appropriate mix of investments is during a market correction which usually come around at regular intervals and is defined by a fall of at least 10% from the previous high point.

Compare Rates of Return

Numerous academic studies over the years have shown that over the long term, investment in stocks & shares have provided a superior return to both cash and bonds. The very long term (since 1900) average for shares, after inflation, is 5% per year compared to around 2% for bonds and just 1% for cash.

According to the latest Barclays Equity Gilt Study (2017), the real returns on equities (after inflation) has significantly outpaced cash savings and government bonds over 5, 10, 50 and even 100 years. For example, **over the past 50 years**, the real return, net of inflation and expressed as annualised % per year was:

equities (shares) 6.0%

govt. bonds (gilts) 3.1%, and

cash deposits 1.3%

In any 20 year period over the past century, equities have provided a better return than bonds 99% of the time. Therefore, over the longer periods, it makes sense to have some degree of exposure to the equity markets, particularly for those younger investors with a longer time frame.

The only problem being, equities are far more volatile than bonds or cash so they can be a bit of a rollercoaster ride - a problem if you are the type of person who frequently monitors the performance of your portfolio.

Looking at different timeframes will produce widely varying results. For example the after-inflation returns for the 10 years to end 2016 the results were -:

equities 2.5%, gilts 4.3%, and cash deposits -1.3%(negative).

Looking at the single year of 2017 and the total return for the FTSE All Share index was over 13% and global equity returns were over 20% partly due to the fall in the value of sterling post Brexit. However in 2018, the returns for all equity markets were negative so in any single year it's really down to a coin toss whether your portfolio will be showing a profit or loss. For many years, cash deposit rates have remained below inflation.

Market Volatility

As we have seen, equities are likely to offer better returns than bonds and cash over the longer periods. However, there is a price to pay for this return - **volatility**. This basically means the value of your investments can rise or fall, sometimes quite dramatically in a short period of time.

This is very different to cash savings in a building society where the amount invested remains exactly the same, leaving aside any interest, over any time period. Therefore £1,000 invested today will remain £1,000 next year and in 5 years or 15 years. There is zero volatility to capital.

It is vitally important for every would-be investor to understand this difference between savings and investing.

Equity and bond markets react constantly to events all around the world - military conflicts, natural disasters, economic and political events - these significant events can trigger large swings in the markets all around the globe.

Over relatively shorter periods of perhaps 1, 2 or 3 years, its really down to more luck than judgment whether your investment will show a positive return. You could be lucky and the markets shoot up and your return in year 1 is 20% - this is not uncommon. Its just as likely the market will drop just after your carefully selected investment has been purchased and you are sitting on a paper loss of 15% - again, not uncommon.

This is market volatility and many newcomers to investing - possibly sucked in during a surge period when the media stories are all about the FTSE hitting record highs as we have witnessed in early 2018 - will be unprepared, they see their hard-earned savings disappearing at a rapid pace as we saw at the end of that year. They may get scared off, sell up and never return - far too risky! Where the FTSE may go in the remainder of 2019 and beyond is unknown.

I have been investing for over 25 years and find it impossible to predict the direction of the markets - whether today is a good point to begin the investment journey is a question only the individual can answer. If I were investing a large lump sum when markets were at an high point, I would think about a strategy to divide up the sum and invest in stages so that I could minimise the possibility of all my investment falling in value when the markets reversed.

It will, of course be less of an issue for those feeding money into the market on a regular monthly basis over the longer periods as they are likely to benefit from the effect of pound cost averaging.

Over the longer periods of at least 5 years and better still 10+ years, the <u>probability</u> of a positive return, whilst not guaranteed, is far more likely. In any 5 yr period over the past 50 years, returns have been positive 9 times out of 10. In any 20 yr period, they have always produced positive returns.

Therefore, if you choose to invest, you really need to be in it for the long haul to give yourself the best chance of a decent return on your capital.

Finally, the term 'risk' is often used sometimes misleadingly used by the financial media as a shorthand for volatility. The two should not however be confused - according to stockmarket legend Warren Buffett **"Risk comes from not knowing what you are doing"** - therefore, make sure you fully understand from the outset what you want to do and how you want to do it. In particular, be sure to understand your temperament and capacity for a sudden downturn in the markets and ensure your asset mix corresponds.

Beware of Constant Monitoring

When we first begin our journey - purchase our investment trust or index tracker - its only natural to keep a close eye on how its getting on.

However, the more we view our portfolio, the more disappointed we will become. This is because, as a species, we appear to be affected far more by a fall in the value of out investment compared to the pleasure or 'feel good' factor we experience from a share price gain.

Over the longer term, the markets have risen, in 2017 the FTSE All Share index was up just over 13% - however on a day to day basis its probably 50:50 whether the markets will be up or down. Therefore if you monitor your portfolio on a daily basis, you are more likely to become unhappy or disillusioned because the cumulative effect of the down days will far outweigh the lesser pleasures of the up days.

To avoid disappointment therefore, it's probably a good idea to steer clear of constant monitoring and review progress maybe once or twice each year.

Pound Cost Averaging

If you invest the same amount of money each month during a period when the markets are high, you will receive fewer units in your chosen investment fund compared to when the markets are lower. The average cost of each monthly purchase will be averaged out over time - less units when the markets are high and more when the markets are lower. This should help to ease any concern as to when is a good time to invest. Investing 'little and often' can be a good way for the would-be investor to build an investment portfolio for the long term.

7. A Diverse Portfolio

We all like to make a little extra money - but if you are anything like me, you hate losing money even more. The best investment strategy of all is the one that guarantees never to lose money - only one problem, such a strategy has yet to be devised.

The next best option therefore would be to limit any potential loss by selecting a diverse range of investments.

As a general rule, its not a good idea to put all your eggs in one basket.

Pooled investment vehicles like investment trusts, exchange traded funds, unit trusts and OEICs, will typically hold one hundred or more individual shares or bonds and these are a simple way to diversify your portfolio.

It is natural to look at the market you are most familiar with - for those in the UK that is the FTSE 100 or FTSE All Share however, the UK accounts for under 10% of the global market. It is usually a good idea to also look at geographic diversity - global funds invest in many markets around the world.

For the average small investor, I would suggest the better returns are more likely to flow from a low cost, well diversified and balanced portfolio.

Indeed with the introduction of new products to the market such as the broadly diversified Vanguard LifeStrategy funds (see later), small investors have the option of a one-stop, no fuss investment vehicle providing all the diversity and balance that may be required.

Asset Allocation

There is much written about this important aspect of investing. Your decision on how to spread your portfolio between various types of asset - equities, bonds, property and cash - will be determined by such factors as your time frame, your degree of comfort in holding the more volatile assets such as equities and your life stage.

If you have cash savings in a building society for example and you decide to invest half of this on the markets, your allocation to cash will be 50%. You then decide how to allocate the remaining 50% between equities, bonds and maybe property or commodities such as gold for example.

There is no such thing as a perfect allocation - the most appropriate model will be the one that most closely fits the temperament and attitude to risk & volatility of the individual. The young buck - usually male - who likes to take risks in the early years will opt mostly for equities - the more conservative minded risk-averse person may choose a more balanced approach 50% equities and 50% bonds. Those who have a shorter time horizon such as perhaps people in retirement may feel more comfortable with a larger percentage in bonds and say 20% or 30% in equities.

We are all at different stages and have differing attitudes to risk so **there is no 'one size fits all'**.

The main points to get across are :

- equities are likely to give a higher return than bonds, but are more volatile

- bonds will probably provide lower returns but greater stability to smooth the ups and downs

Of course, there are other assets available - commodities such as gold, commercial property etc. which some investors may like to include in the mix.

A sensible asset allocation is not so much about maximising returns, but more about meshing your chosen mix of investments with your personality. It's akin to building a robust boat that will ride out the stormy waters of the global markets and get you from A to B.

Risk Profile & Volatility

When first starting out on the investing journey, I believe one of the least understood aspects is probably the need for every investor to understand their unique emotional make up and ability to withstand the volatility of the markets and then to match this to the most appropriate allocation of assets taking into account time horizon.

Successful investing is all about the long term so it is vitally important to 'stay in the game' for many years. It is therefore important at the start of the process to find an investment strategy that meshes well with your personality and temperament.

This is where asset allocation comes into play. Some assets such as equities and commodities are far more volatile than other more stable assets such as cash and government bonds (gilts). Investors who invest 100% in equities are likely to get the higher returns over the longer periods BUT are more likely to throw in the towel when their portfolio loses 20% of its value in the blink of an eye…and go on to lose a further 25% over the following year.

Work Out a Suitable Starting Allocation

There are many models and online tools around to help with this.

A site I sometimes use is Vanguard's asset mixer which provides a visual image of how returns may be affected over time using various allocation percentages - equities/bonds/cash.

In my experience however, it should not be too difficult to understand your temperament - cautious type, balanced, adventurous etc. and then decide upon a simple mix of equities, bonds, cash and possibly property.

Younger, more adventurous investors may decide that they can handle the ups and downs of the markets in the early years and therefore choose an allocation of 80% or even100% equities based on the premise they will provide the better returns over the next 20 to 30 years. This is a perfectly viable and logical decision - provided they are the sort of person who can stick with it.

Other more cautious investors may decide to go down the less volatile route and select a classic allocation mix of 60% equities and 40% bonds. They may wish to include 10% property and reduce the equity sector or they may like to hold

5% in commodities such as gold. There are no right or wrong decisions.

Maybe you can take some guidance from Vanguard's recently launched Target Retirement Funds. Based upon a retirement age of 65, the equity allocation for younger people is 80% to age 43 years which is gradually reduced to 50% at age 68 yrs and to 30% at age 75 yrs.

Their more conservative analysis starts with 70% equities to age 43 yrs, reduces to 40% by age 67 yrs and then just 20% equities at age 75 yrs.

Tim Hale, author of **'Smarter Investing'** has suggested a formula of 4% equities for each year you intend to invest - this is roughly the allocation I decided was right for me. In the early years, I was more or less 100% invested in stocks & shares, but now I am in my 60s this has been reduced to around 60% equities as more government bonds and fixed income has been gradually introduced.

Therefore, it is advisable to give some careful consideration to this area during the planning process. As your investing progresses and you become more experienced, it is always possible to review your initial allocation decision. If you are finding your starting allocation is too volatile and causing you a degree of stress then make an adjustment by reducing the equity proportion by say 10% and increase bonds.

Finally, do not get overly bogged down with 3.5% here and 6.3% there - a broad brush approach will be easier to manage, easier to rebalance and will get the job done.

When all is said and done, the "best" strategy in relation to allocation of assets is the one that you understand, feel comfortable with and importantly, **can stick with in good times and bad over your selected timeframe.**

Rebalancing & Mean Reversion

Markets move in cycles - often lasting for several years, maybe a decade. Sometimes equities will be ahead, at other points in the cycle, bonds will be doing well.

Over the longer terms, the average between the high points and low points for any asset class can be plotted or calculated and the movements towards this average is called mean reversion. Whilst these cycles are easy to identify in retrospect, it is not easy for the average investor (or professional) to correctly identify the turning point of these cycles. If it were easy, you just invest your money at the low point of the equity cycle and move into bonds when they hit the high point of the cycle - simples! In the real world, markets frequently overshoot or undershoot their long-term average for quite some time.

The point of building a diverse portfolio of equities and bonds is to try and reduce volatility. Reducing volatility of a portfolio can help the investor to 'stay in the game' for the longer periods. The two types of asset class rarely move in tandem - as one sector of the market is booming, another will be going through a difficult time. Rebalancing your portfolio, say once per year, involves selling some of the assets which have done well and reinvesting the proceeds into the sectors which have underperformed.

Example : Say you decide upon a classic mix of 60% equities and 40% bonds for your portfolio asset allocation.

The initial investment is £10,000 so you have £6,000 invested in stocks & shares and £4,000 in government bonds. It is a good year for shares and by the end of year 1, the value of the equities have increased to £8,000. Its not such a great year for bonds and the value for them remains unchanged at £4,000.

This means your total portfolio has risen in value due to the equities and is now worth £12,000. The allocation has changed from 60:40 to become 67% equities and 33% bonds. It is out of balance from your starting allocation.

Rebalancing involves an adjustment to the new mix to bring them back to the original allocation. Therefore, to rebalance, you will sell 7% of the equities and reinvest this money into the bonds thereby restoring the allocation to 60:40 - the £12,000 portfolio now comprises £7,200 equities and £4,800 bonds.

The only sensible reason to do this is because of the investing principle known as **reversion to mean**. Some of the gain from the sector which has done well is siphoned off into the sector which has not done so well. In the above example, some of the gains from the equities are 'banked' in the expectation that when the cycles reverse, the gain will be used to benefit bonds which are likely to move up as equities move down.

Whilst many forms of investments, including equities, can trade above or below their long term average - often for surprisingly lengthy periods - in the long term, they always move back in line with that average sooner or later.

Rebalancing of a portfolio can be done at any regular interval but I would suggest not too frequently - a common time frame might be once per year of even every two years. Alternatively it can be done when one asset class is above a certain amount - say 5% or 10% above/below the starting allocation.

If you are the sort of investor who can handle large market swings, then 100% equities may be the way to go in which case there is no rebalancing required, however most investors would be better advised to consider a more balanced and diverse portfolio.

Of course, it can be a bit of a chore to carry out the rebalancing of your portfolio or it can be forgotten. Therefore, any option which offers to automatically rebalance - such as with the Vanguard LifeStrategy funds (see later), will be a bonus.

Climate Change

Whilst on the subject of market risks, this may be appropriate time to introduce a section on the possible impact of climate change in relation to investments. This must surely be the defining issue of our time and we are at, or very close to, a defining moment. Each year we see news stories of more wildfires around the world, more extreme hurricanes and flooding. I read reports on the subject from the IPCC and the more I delve, the more concerned I become so in 2019 I thought it would be appropriate to add this short section to my books.

Unless some very fundamental changes are made to combat climate change, we are currently on track to increase global temperatures by a further 3 or 4 degrees C by the end of this century. As the risks become more apparent, investors will need to be prepared for greater regulation from governments as they attempt to meet their carbon reduction targets.

Investing will be affected by the global impact on our economies if climate change is not addressed in time and therefore the reader must take a view on whether they accept the warnings from the climate change scientists, and if so, whether they think the global community is able to make the changes required within the timeframe of their investing horizon.

Personally, I think many areas of business will be impacted by run-away climate change - oil & gas, airlines, property and real estate, utilities, insurance, travel & leisure, banks and car manufacturing to name just a few in the front line.

Some people say we have probably left it too late to make the changes required and that we are now past the point of no return. Others are more optimistic and suggest we still have a window of around 10 or 15 years to make the big changes required to avoid a doomsday scenario. Indeed there are many examples all around the world that transformation is taking place, attitudes and behaviours are changing. In the UK in 2018, the capacity of renewables such as wind and solar has overtaken coal and gas for the first time. Renewables are expected to provide over 50% of UK energy needs by 2020. The World Bank has doubled its funding to $200 billion to tackle climate change. The world's biggest polluter China has already met its targets under the Paris Agreement as it has made some radical changes to reduce reliance on coal and switch to renewables. The world's largest shipping company Maersk has pledged to ditch fossil fuels and is switching to more sustainable carbon-neutral energy efficient solutions.

The solutions will involve the complete phasing out of coal-fired power, a move to electric transport, a big reduction in fossil fuel dependence such as oil and gas and a shift to renewable energy.

Climate change is clearly a big issue and will not be going away so it is something investors need to think about. Some sectors will be adversely affected unless they can adapt their business model quickly. On the flip side, there will be sectors which will benefit such as technology which can address and help to minimise the effects of global warming.

I do not know how things will develop or specifically how the markets will adapt and respond to the threats, but I do know that climate change will bring risks but also opportunities. Investing over the coming 5 or 10 years may not be too adversely affected but it seems sensible to take some sort of view on climate change when deciding on a plan for longer periods, say the next 20 or 30 years.

Personally, I am optimistic we can rise to the challenge but I do not underestimate the scale of the changes we all need to make in the transition towards a more sustainable world system.

8. Keep Costs to a Minimum

For me, and I am sure many other small investors, the costs associated with investing are a very important consideration - arguably they can affect long term returns even more so than asset allocation. To get the best returns from your self directed efforts, it is essential to keep costs as low as possible - this involves broker/platform costs, fund charges and trading fees.

Investors have no control over the markets but they can control the fees they pay on their choice of investments and also their choice of broker.

Fund Charges

In his book **"Monkey with a Pin"** (free download from Amazon) Pete Comley suggests the average investor could be missing out on up to 6% in returns on their investments. His research points to around 2% of this being attributed to charges.

Fundsmith manager Terry Smith says the average UK investor who invests via an adviser, uses a platform and then invests in managed funds, incurs total charges of about 3% each year.

Managed investment fund total charges range between 0.5% and 2.5%. Typically around 0.75% - 1.25% is the ongoing charges rate for many depending on the class of fund selected. However, these charges which appear in all the literature and comparison tables are not the whole story.

Although they are called 'total expense ratio - TER' or now 'ongoing charges figure - OCF' - surprisingly, they do not include all the charges levied on the fund. For a start, they do not include transaction charges for the buying and selling of shares within the fund - nor do they include the 0.5% stamp duty on the purchases.

The average 'churn' or portfolio turnover rate every year is, around 50% - that means half of the shares held in the portfolio are likely to be traded in any given year. With some funds, the churn rate can be as high as 200% - which means the whole portfolio is turned over every 6 months. For every 10% of portfolio turnover, at least 0.20% is added in additional hidden charges. This will typically add an extra 1% to the advertised costs of holding the fund - and probably more for less liquid markets like smaller companies and emerging markets funds.

The effect of these **'hidden extras'** will mean the average retail investor is paying not 0.75% or 1.0% in charges but possibly as high as 2% or even 3%. That's 2% - 3% every year on the total value of your investments - whether they have performed well or not. For a typical small investors holding of £25,000 the additional charges could be £500 **every year**.

Over the years, there has been extensive studies and research that shows, over an extended period, most fund managers fail to consistently beat their chosen benchmark. Research also shows that many small investors continue to waste money by paying active management fees for this consistent failure.

This underperformance is not just due to poor asset allocation or stock selection, though this is a factor, but just as much the drag effect of the high charges affecting the fund performance.

To see a visual illustration of how various levels of charges impact investment returns over various periods visit the Vanguard tools website www.vanguard.co.uk/uk/portal/investor-resources/learning/tools#Cost

Brokers Platform Charges

In addition to fund charges, investors will also need to factor in the costs of platform charges levied by the online broker who holds your portfolio of investments.

Investment providers broadly fall into two groups:

those that charge a **percentage fee** which are obviously good if you have smaller amounts invested - probably the norm for most investors in the early years,

and those that charge a **flat fee** which is possibly the better choice for larger sums.

To help with the selection process, there are a couple of useful comparison sites :

Monevator.com - 'Compare Brokers' (see Investing tab)

Comparefundplatforms.com - provides an interactive process

When working through this selection process, it will be useful to have a clear idea whether you will be using mainly tracker funds (unit trusts or OEICs) or mainly ETFs (also including the option to hold individual shares and investment trusts), as some brokers will charge different rates. For example, with one of my own brokers, AJ Bell Youinvest, the platform fee for holding investments in my ISA is currently 0.25% p.a. but there is a cap of £30 per annum for holdings of investment trusts, ETFs and shares.

Equally, some brokers may offer a better deal for SIPP investors whilst others may be better for ISA investors.

A good strategy for the novice investor is to start with a provider with a low percentage fee, ideally less than 0.30% and also one that does not levy a charge for buying/selling funds if you are building a portfolio via regular monthly contributions. As a general rule of thumb, when the value of the portfolio gets above £30,000 to £35,000 point, it will be worthwhile comparing the costs of the flat fee provider.

Some of the more popular online brokers would be Hargreaves Lansdown, AJ Bell YouInvest, Vanguard Investor, iWeb, Charles Stanley Direct, Halifax Share Dealing (links at end of book).

Cost of Holding Low Cost Trackers

As more people start to understand the drag effect of these higher fund and/or platform charges on their investment performance, they are increasingly turning to low cost passive tracker funds. According to Investment Management Association figures, trackers accounted for around 14% of the UK private investor market in 2016. In the USA, index funds accounted for over 30% of the market in 2017 and it is expected they will overtake actively managed funds by 2023.

Charges are typically in the region of 0.25% or less - the Vanguard FTSE UK Equity Index for example has charges of just 0.08% (plus 0.4% one-off dilution levy). Portfolio turnover rate is much lower on trackers - typically around the 10% - 15% range so the total charges for this should be in the region of an additional 0.20%.

Alternatively, Vanguard offer a FTSE 100 ETF (exchange traded fund) with charges of 0.10%.

The difference between say ~0.40% total costs for a tracker and ~2.0% or more real total costs on a managed fund will have a huge impact on returns.

Lets take the example of a person with a £10,000 lump sum and investing £100 per month over 30 years - a total investment of £46,000. Assume an average annual return of 6% p.a.

With the managed fund, after 30 years the investment would be worth **£101,185** and with the low cost tracker **£142,389** (comparison via Candid Money). That's a difference of £41,204 - over 40% going into your pocket rather than the fund manager.

Tax Efficient Investing

Many people will be familiar with a cash ISA offered by banks and building societies. Just as the interest on cash can be protected from the taxman, so can investments in a stocks & shares ISA or pension.

1. ISA

ISAs are merely a wrapper - anything inside this wrapper is out of reach of the taxman. Every adult can invest up to £20,000 (2019/20) each year in either a cash ISA or a stocks & shares ISA (S&S) or a combination of the two.

There are usually no extra costs involved to invest in a S&S ISA compared to a normal trading account (non-ISA) so, even where there is no immediate advantage, it will be always be worthwhile using a S&S ISA in my opinion.

Once a self-select S&S ISA has been opened, the investor can hold many different types of investment within it - shares, bonds, index funds, collectives, multi-index etc.

Investing in a S&S ISA is a two stage process - first you select the broker/platform and secondly, you then fund your ISA and decide which investments to purchase. It's a bit like doing the weekly shop - first you decide which supermarket - Tesco, Aldi, Asda etc. Having decided on one, you then go round with your trolley selecting the groceries.

2. New Lifetime ISA

From April 2017 anyone between the ages of 18 and 40 yrs can save as much or as little as they wish up to a maximum of £4,000 per annum. For savings up to the age of 50 yrs, the government will add a 25% bonus i.e a max. of £1,000 at the end of each year.

The money can be used towards the deposit for a first home worth up to £450,000 or can be saved as a nest egg for retirement and taken tax-free from the age of 60 yrs. Unlike pension savings, withdrawals can be taken at any time before 60 yrs subject to the loss of bonus and also a penalty charge.

Therefore someone contributing the maximum from their 18th birthday could save £128,000 by the age of 50 yrs and receive total bonuses of £32,000.

Assuming a modest return on investment of 5% and taking into account platform/fund charges of 0.5%, the pot would grow to around £350,000 by age 50 yrs and the with no further contributions, to £543,000 by the age of 60 yrs.

3. Pension

For the sake of completeness, I will mention pensions but they are quite a large area of investment in their own right and I have covered this subject more fully in my book **'DIY Pensions'**.

Like S&S ISAs, they are merely a wrapper within which to hold investments in a tax efficient way. The big advantage over ISAs is that with a pension, for every £100 you put in, the taxman will throw in a further £25 so your investment pot will grow much quicker than in an ISA.

The drawback is that you cannot get at the pension money until age 55 yrs (from 2028 rises to 57 yrs) whereas with your ISA you can access your money anytime.

The easiest type of pension to operate on a DIY basis is the self-invested personal pension or SIPP. In fact it operates in much the same way as described above. Most low cost brokers such as Hargreaves Lansdown, AJ Bell Youinvest,

Charles Stanley Direct etc. will offer platforms to operate a S&S ISA as well as SIPP.

4. Taxation of Savings Interest & Dividends

From April 2016, interest from savings is no longer taxed at source. There is now a personal savings allowance and everyone can receive up to £1,000 tax free interest for basic rate taxpayers (£500 for higher rate taxpayers) on their cash savings and in addition, they can also receive up to £2,000 tax free on any dividends from investments (2018/19).

9. Active -v- Passive

In the previous chapter, we looked at the importance of keeping costs as low as possible.

Most of the time, I would say the better return over the longer period will come from the lower cost index fund or ETF. However, if the actively managed fund can generate better returns than the low cost tracker then it would be worth considering paying the extra charges which may amount to 1% or thereabouts. So, lets investigate the evidence for active fund managers out-performing low cost passive index funds.

First of all, a definition.

Active investing is an attempt by the fund manager, using his/her skill, judgement and research, to produce a better than average return. The funds they manage will usually be assessed by reference to a benchmark - for example, a UK fund might offer to outperform the FTSE All Share Index - that is all the shares on the London stock exchange. The majority of funds and investment trusts - 90% or so of the overall market - are actively managed.

By contrast, a **passive** approach using index tracker funds, involves no fund manager. The fund will usually hold all the constituents of a particular index which it is set up to track. For example, a FTSE 100 tracker will hold all 100 shares which make up the FTSE 100 Index. A tracker providing exposure to the USA might track the S&P 500 - the 500 largest shares trading on the US stock exchange.

Some tracker funds will provide a very wide, diversified exposure such as a global fund which may hold over 2,000 shares listed on many different stock exchanges all around the world. Other trackers may be more focussed on a particular sub-sector of the market and hold maybe 30 or 40 shares. There are well over 100 markets to track and include equities, fixed interest, commodities such as gold, as well as different sectors and sub-sectors of the market.

Although there is always much debate as to which approach provides the better returns for investors, one aspect cannot be disputed - as we have seen earlier, most passive trackers have much lower charges than most active funds.

The Research

In recent years, some of the best financial brains in the financial world have crunched the statistics and have come down firmly in favour of index funds. Over the longer periods, say 10 years +, there are many academic studies which show the average low cost tracker will out-perform the average managed fund.

Former hedge fund manager Lars Kroijer recommends passive funds as the most logical choice for any investor in his book **'Investing Demystified'**. I can recommend the video series (free) based on the book at the author's website www.kroijer.com.

Another UK focussed classic is Tim Hale's **'Smarter Investing'** which also comes down firmly in the camp of the passive index approach. Both of the above are well worth a read for those who wish to explore investing in greater detail.

Legendary US investor Warren Buffett repeatedly suggests that the average small investor would be best served by low cost index tracker funds. He recently revealed that when he passes away, he has left instructions in his will for the bulk of his estate to be placed into Vanguard index funds for the benefit of his wife.

According to a report from S&P Dow Jones Indices, over half the actively managed UK equity funds underperformed their benchmark index in 2014. In the 3 year period to December 2014, over 80% of both global equity and US equity funds underperformed their respective index.

One of the big reasons most fund managers fail to beat their benchmark consistently is the effect of fund charges - as we have seen, typical total costs will average around 2% every year which is a big drag on performance - whether the manager is good, bad or indifferent, the funds all seem to charge the same ongoing charges.

Vanguard Study

A study published by Vanguard (April 2014) of 6,500 funds available in the UK found that if they are split in half between high and low cost, the cheaper ones outperformed in 9 out of 11 investment categories in the 10 years to the end of 2013.

Vanguard has also carried out research which found that high costs were one of several reasons why the majority of actively managed funds underperformed their chosen benchmarks. The study suggests that 64% of active equity managers underperformed their benchmarks over the 15-year period until 2014, while more than 87% of global bond managers underperformed their benchmarks over the same period.

This latest research seems to underline many previous academic studies which show that lower cost funds perform better than higher cost funds.

www.vanguard.co.uk/documents/portal/press_releases/low-cost-funds-more-likely-to-outperform-higher-cost-funds.pdf

The Star Manager

Of course, there are always the exception to the rule and it cannot be denied there are some fund managers who consistently perform well - Nick Train springs to mind as one who has done very well for his investors over many years. The problem is that for the investor just starting out, how are they supposed to find the handful of managers who will perform well for the many years ahead from the thousands of funds available?

For every star manager like Train who can consistently deliver the goods, there are many, many more who fail to deliver consistent, above-average returns - indeed some funds are little more than closet trackers, achieving poor or average returns but charging much the same fees as the genuine star managers.

The choice for would-be investors would therefore be between selecting a fund from the several thousands on offer with maybe a 10% chance of the manager delivering an above-average return or the alternative - you can choose a low cost tracker with a 100% chance of matching the index.

On a personal level, I have held a mixture of managed investment trusts for many years. I did some research recently to compare the returns of my investment trusts portfolio against a low cost Vanguard tracker fund - the comparison was only over a five year period which is not long in investing horizons but even so, the tracker fund came out ahead. I have been missing out on maybe 1% or 2% return over recent years which may not seem like a significant amount - indeed it probably is not - but over the longer periods, these small percentages will compound and result in a sizable sum.

Unsurprisingly, I have revised my personal investing strategy in recent years to embrace a much larger proportion of low cost index funds.

For those wishing to explore more aspects of passive investing I recommend starting with some of the excellent articles on Monevator :

http://monevator.com/category/investing/passive-investing-investing/

Also worth a look - The Evidence-Based Investor

http://www.evidenceinvestor.co.uk/evidence/

Conclusion

Some investors will prefer a more active approach and some will prefer the low cost index approach. Some investors, myself included, will use a mixture of both. The active -v- passive debate will no doubt continue to run as the evidence and research to support one side or the other is presented from time to time.

For those who may wish to conduct further research, there is much material available via the internet - finding a definitive answer from someone who does not have a financial interest one way or the other is possibly more elusive.

As a general rule, for me, the lower cost funds - active or passive, will usually provide the better returns for the average small investor compared to the higher cost funds over time. For a simple, no frills buy-and-forget approach, I believe most investors will benefit from a low cost, globally diverse and balanced index fund.

10. The Humble Index Tracker

When I started my investing journey in the late 1980s, the low cost tracker funds were just starting to emerge in the UK. Although they had been available in the USA since the concept was introduced by founder of Vanguard, John Bogle in the 1970s, it was some years later before the insurer Legal & General launched their UK index fund in the early 1990s.

Index or passive investing revolves around the view that it is difficult for fund managers to consistently outperform the market over the long term - though undoubtedly a few do manage this - so attempting to match its performance by tracking it as closely as possible is the more logical approach. These passive products have a very simple objective - follow an index's performance as closely as possible but don't add to effort or cost in trying to beat it.

This approach cuts down on research and trading costs, meaning trackers tend to have a natural head start ahead of their more expensive managed rivals.

A passive approach frees investors from the task of fund selection and eliminates manager risk. This means that basically their returns will be largely determined by just two elements - **asset allocation** combined with the **costs** of the fund selected to track the required sector of the market.

What Are They?

There are many markets around the world where shares, bonds and other types of security such as commodities can be traded. In the UK we have the FTSE which is divided into several different sectors. The FTSE 100 index for example represents the largest 100 companies.

As the individual shares are bought and sold each day, their market value changes. These changes are averaged out to create the FTSE 100 index. To gain access to the FTSE 100, you could of course, buy all the individual shares which are currently in the top 100. This would not however be very practical as you would have to pay dealing costs for each individual purchase - at £10 a pop, this would cost £1,000 for starters.

Also, as time passes, some companies lose market value whilst others are on the up, therefore the top 100 companies are constantly changing and the index reflects this periodically when some constituents leave the index and others take their place.

For investors who decide they would like exposure to this sector of the UK market, the easiest and most cost effective way is to purchase just one low cost tracker which follows the FTSE 100 index. There is no dealing fee to purchase such a tracker fund with some brokers.

How Do They Track the Index?

There are two main ways to mimic the index - full replication and partial replication.

Full replication is where the fund acquires all the shares in the index, for example the FTSE 100.

Where it would be difficult to buy all the shares, some funds will hold a representative sample. The global index for example comprises over 1,700 shares from over 20 countries - full replication may prove too costly and be detrimental to the performance of the fund.

Structure

Passive investors typically make use of two kinds of fund - the traditional unit trust funds or open-ended investment company OEICs (together often referred to as funds). There are usually two options of each fund available - accumulation units (acc) and income units (inc). The former are more suitable for those building for the future and who do not require immediate income to be paid - all income received is automatically reinvested within the fund and this will be reflected in the pricing of the units.

Income units will usually be more suitable for investors who may wish to take a regular income from their investments. The income from the fund is therefore paid out and will remain as cash in the investors account until withdrawn or reinvested.

The second common way to holding trackers is via exchange-traded funds (ETFs).

Traditional tracker funds do not normally incur the dealing costs that ETFs do when they are traded. Therefore they are usually better suited where investments are being fed into building a portfolio on a monthly basis e.g. £100 p.m. ETFs often give access to niche areas of the market and can be used to make quick and tactical portfolio changes.

Who Provides Them?

There are many providers of index funds - some of the larger, more popular providers would be Vanguard, BlackRock, Legal & General, Fidelity and HSBC

ETF providers include BlackRock iShares, Vanguard and State Street SPDR

It will be possible to hold investments with some of the providers direct. For example in 2017, Vanguard Investor launched its own retail platform with platform charges of just 0.15% per year. Therefore if you hold investments to the value of £10,000 the annual platform fee would be just £15. At the present time you can only hold Vanguard funds/ETFs so it would not be suitable for those wishing to hold products from other providers. Other options will be to have an account with a low cost DIY platform/broker where you are free to mix and match whatever index fund or ETF tracker you want from any provider.

Here's a link to my blog article **'Selecting Your Online Broker'**

http://diyinvestoruk.blogspot.co.uk/2016/05/selecting-your-diy-online-broker.html

11. The Simple, All-in-One Options

In previous chapters I have covered a few important areas of investing which I hope will provide the reader with some context and a simple rationale for the investing process combined with some of my basics for a better chance of a successful outcome.

We have seen the advantages of investing over the longer term horizon, how mixing bonds with equities can lower volatility to give investors a better opportunity to 'stay the course' and the importance of keeping the costs of investing to a minimum.

In recent years, I have become increasingly attracted to the benefits that a low cost passive tracker can offer to the DIY investor. Indeed, my personal investing strategy has evolved and I now hold a significant proportion of my ISA portfolio in Vanguard LifeStrategy funds.

John Bogle is a pioneer of index investing and he set up Vanguard in the 1970s - it has grown rapidly and is today one of the worlds largest investment managers with around 20 million investors and over $5 trillion of global assets under their management. Vanguard are a mutual company which means the funds they operate are owned by their investors.

They offer a range of options including funds and ETFs. They launched their LifeStrategy funds on the UK market in 2011 and these funds offer a low cost, diversified one-stop investing solution. Most importantly however, I believe the simple concept they provide can be understood and implemented by anyone who has decided to invest for the long term.

As readers of my blog will know, I have incorporated these funds into my ISA portfolio as I believe they will offer a little more global diversity combined with lower costs compared to some of my UK focussed investment trusts. They also provide me with a smoother ride by offering much less volatility compared to some of my equity-only technology investments.

Of course, this must not be taken as a recommendation - each investor should satisfy themselves that any particular investment is suitable for their individual situation or circumstances.

The One Stop Options

A. LifeStrategy

The essence of the Vanguard LifeStrategy (LS) funds are their simplicity. They are a family of five ready-made portfolios which have each been professionally constructed from Vanguard's underlying index funds - some equity and some bonds.

They range from LS20 to LS100 according to the level of equities required by the investor. For example, the LS40 will have 40% equities and 60% bonds; the LS80 will have 80% equities and 20% bonds.

All the investor needs to do is decide what level of exposure to equities they feel comfortable with. It will always be possible to move to a lower (or higher) level at any point should the investor need a different level of equity/bond mix. It will always be possible to hold two funds e.g. LS40 and LS60 to give a 50:50 mix if required.

The LS range offers instant diversification, automatic rebalancing and low costs - ongoing charges of 0.22%.

The equities element will hold a mix of globally diversified shares including UK FTSE, Europe, USA, Japan, Asia and some emerging markets. The bond element (assuming you do not want the 100% equity) will comprise a combination of UK gilts, global bonds, corporate bonds and inflation-linked gilts.

As we have seen earlier, the average long term returns on equities have been significantly higher than bonds or cash. This will be reflected in the level of LS fund selected - the LS80 holds a higher proportion of equities to the LS40 and the investor would therefore expect better long-term returns from the LS80.

The LifeStrategy funds have been available in the UK since June 2011 - at the end of 2018 the average annualised return for each level of LS fund are as follows :

LifeStrategy 20   **5.32%** p.a.

LifeStrategy 40   **6.43%** p.a.

LifeStrategy 60   **7.48%** p.a.

LifeStrategy 80   **8.46%** p.a.

LifeStrategy100   **9.36%** p.a.

At the time of publication, the most popular fund is the LifeStrategy 60 with £4.2bn in assets. If a sum of £1,000 was invested at the launch, it would now be worth £1,720 (excluding platform costs).

The period since 2011 has been fairly positive for global markets recovering after the severe meltdown of 2008/09. However markets do not rise in a straight line and as we have seen in the final quarter of 2018, the sell-off can be quite dramatic. Furthermore, the returns for 2016 were boosted by the fall in the value of sterling following the UK referendum vote to leave the EU.

The average returns listed above represent a period of 7.5 years and should give some indication of the likely returns to be expected for future periods but bearing in mind that any one year can vary widely from the longer term averages. Take the Lifestrategy 80 fund for example, the annual return for 2018 was a loss of -4.0% whereas the longer term average since 2011 has been 8.5% p.a.

The strategy of using globally diverse investments will always come with foreign exchange considerations as many non-UK investments will typically be priced in US dollars. A fall in sterling will generally provide a positive boost to investments priced in dollars and this was apparent in 2016, but when the pound rises it will have the reverse effect.

These returns are frequently updated so anyone can visit the Vanguard Investor website to check the current figures for the fund they may interested in researching.

https://www.vanguardinvestor.co.uk/

Putting together a DIY investment portfolio does not come much simpler than this. You decide on your asset allocation and then choose your corresponding LifeStrategy fund(s), select your low cost broker, set up your automated monthly direct debit - job done, get on with your life!

For those who think this method may be suitable for their own strategy and who wish to conduct further research, here's a link to Vanguard's LifeStrategy page -

www.vanguard.co.uk/documents/portal/literature/lifestrategy-brochure-retail.pdf

B. Target Retirement

As the name suggests, the Target Retirement funds are designed for the pension market. They are similar to the Lifestrategy funds and were introduced to the UK market in May 2016.

Each fund has a target date - 2035, 2040, 2055 etc. and the investor simple selects the year from which they intend to start retirement.

With the LifeStrategy funds, the investor selects the option which most closely matches the desired exposure to equities and Vanguard will automatically rebalance the fund to ensure it remains at the required level. With the target retirement funds, this mix between equities and bonds is not fixed but changes over the life of the fund. Investors pick the fund that best aligns with their expected retirement date, which automatically adjusts its portfolio mix based on the investor's age, shifting towards an increasingly conservative position in later years.

In the early years to mid 40s with over 20 yrs to retirement, the funds are 80% global equities and 20% bonds (similar to the LS80 fund). Thereafter the portfolio gradually reduces the equity percentage and increases the bonds so that at age 68 years the mix is 50:50 then by age 75 yrs the equities are reduced to 30% and the bonds are 70%.

As the name suggests, they are aimed mainly at those wishing to save over the longer term. Vanguard research showed that many investors did not have the time or interest to dedicate to retirement planning. Not everyone will know whether they will take lump sums, a regular income or buy an annuity until they actually reach retirement. These funds help people to save and invest for retirement regardless of how they choose to use the funds in retirement.

Other Options

I have used the Vanguard funds merely as an example as these are the funds provider I use for my personal portfolio and therefore the ones I am most familiar with. Of course, there are similar all-in-one index options offered by other providers such as :

BlackRock's Consensus funds,

HSBC Global Strategy funds and

Legal & General's Multi-Index funds.

Finally, the multi-index funds should not be confused with multi-asset funds - the latter are also a possibility as an all-in-one solution for those who may require a wider selection of assets in a single fund. These might include property, commodities such as gold for example and also cash. These are mostly managed funds and the manager will have flexibility on how the assets are mixed and will move the balance of each asset to reflect his/her view on future prospects for each category. The risk for investors is obviously they are relying on the manager to make consistently good calls between the proportion of the various assets and mix. The multi-asset funds on average tend to be more expensive than the low cost index funds with typical charges of 0.6% - 1.50%.

A full range of multi-asset funds with performance figures can be found under the appropriate tab at Trustnet. Various funds are categorised according to level of equity - such as Mixed Investment 0 - 35% shares, 20 - 60% shares, 40 - 85% shares and Flexible.

https://www2.trustnet.com/Investments/MultiManagerMixedAsset.aspx?univ=O

A Lifetime Solution

I believe the all-in-one investing strategy can be used during the early years when you will be feeding your savings into the investment on a regular basis - most commonly monthly contributions. It could equally be appropriate in the later years when you may be retired and wish to use the accumulated fund for its original purpose as set out in your strategy plans.

The process will be equally valid whether investing into a stocks & shares ISA, Lifetime ISA or a pension SIPP.

Lets take a brief look at each of these two main life stages of investing. I will sketch a brief practical example of a typical scenario for both.

The Early Years

The sooner you can start, the more time your investments have to grow and compound.

In my book "**DIY Pensions**", I described the situation of two people, Alex and Sue. Sue started paying £2,000 per annum into her pension in her 20s and continued for just 10 years then stopped. Alex started paying the same amount 10 years later than Sue and continued for 30 years. Sue paid in a total of £20,000 and Alex paid in a total of £60,000. **At retirement, Sue's pension pot was £100,000 more than Alex's!**

I must admit, when I first came across this illustration, I could hardly believe it was true but I have since done some calculations via the Candid Money site and have verified the figures are correct. This demonstrates the power of compounding returns over a longer period.

Asset Allocation

You will have given some consideration to this aspect during the planning process. For those who are saving for retirement long term, they may go for the Target Retirement option where asset allocation is taken care of automatically and is not therefore an issue.

For those who prefer the LifeStrategy option they will need to choose a fund which most closely matches their temperament and personal circumstances. Everyone should have some idea of a suitable allocation but for those who are uncertain, I would suggest it is better to start with a cautious allocation and make adjustments at a later stage - personally, if I was starting out today in my 20s or 30s, with perhaps 30+ years of investing ahead of me, I would be looking mainly at global equities to do the heavy lifting as they provide the better potential long term returns for my portfolio.

The core of my investments would therefore be focussed on the Vanguard LS80 fund - accumulation units. Some people may feel a more aggressive allocation is appropriate - LS100. Others may decide a more cautious approach would suit them better - therefore LS60, LS40 or an equal combination of the two to produce a 50:50 allocation.

I would set up a direct debit with my chosen broker (see earlier) and arrange a set monthly sum. The broker would most likely be one that offers low charges e.g. below 0.30% and also does not make a charge for the monthly purchase of additional units. At the same time I would set up an automated plan for the monthly contributions to be purchasing units in the LS fund. The more the whole process is automated, the less the investor has to do - I like to keep it simple.

That's just about all there is to it! Job done - get on with life.

Core/Satellite Strategy

Some investors like to use a dual approach to their investing. They have a 'core' of stable long term holdings at the centre of their portfolio. This could account for maybe 60 to 80% of the portfolio value. Around this is the smaller elements which could be used for niche areas such as biotech funds, ethical funds to help the environment or technology trusts for example. Some investors like to 'tinker' from time to time and this strategy allows the investor to maintain a central element which remains untouched whilst changes can be made around the edges which will not cause too much damage if the changes do not work out as planned.

For those who may want to use the LifeStrategy or Target Retirement funds as a core holding, there is always the option to add other investments around it. The LS fund does not include property for example so an additional fund could be added if this was important to the individual who may wish to provide some further diversity.

It is also possible to include managed funds or investment trusts in the same portfolio as the LS index funds should the investor choose to do so although there is no guarantee of any better returns. I hold several investment trusts which have served me well over many years and try to post an annual update for each trust on my blog. I also post an annual review covering all investments at the end of each year.

Scenario 1
Rob is a 28 yr old graphic designer on a salary of £35,000 p.a. He already has the benefit of a company pension provided by his employer. He is saving in a building society for a deposit on a house purchase but he has decided he would like to start a DIY stocks & shares ISA for the longer term.

He feels comfortable with a fairly aggressive asset allocation and decides the most appropriate fund will be the LS80. He will start saving 10% of his gross income and therefore has £300 per month to put in the S&S ISA.

He has looked at the options for a broker and decides to open an account with Vanguard Investor as they do not charge a transaction fee for purchasing on a regular monthly basis. Their platform charges are reasonable at 0.15% which means for each annual contribution of £3,600 he invests, he will be charged £5.00 p.a.

He opens an account online, selects the Vanguard LS80(acc) for regular monthly purchase and sets up a direct debit with his bank for the £300 per month to be automatically transferred to his Vanguard account.

He will make a note to review the level of contributions at the same time each year.

The Later Years

At some stage of your strategy plan - maybe your 50s or 60s - you will look at options for retirement. Its time to take stock and look at the next phase of the plan.

Preservation of Capital

You may have been saving and/or investing for 20, 30 or even 40 years. If so, you will possible have a significant accumulation of capital. As the years pass, many people will be adjusting the investment tilt towards further reducing volatility and generating some extra income from that capital.

If you have not adjusted the level of equity holding in your LifeStrategy fund before now, I would personally be looking to take a step or two back from the equity-heavy LS80 for example, and moving to the LS60 or LS40 - these funds have a lower proportion of equity and a corresponding higher percentage of bonds so they should be more stable.

Options for Taking Income

Unfortunately the natural yield on the LS funds is quite modest - currently (Jan 2019) averaging around 1.5%.

Of course you could invest in a range of income-focussed investment trusts which would generate a natural income yield of around 3.5% - 4% but this would not be generally regarded as a simple process. For those investors who may want to consider this option, it is described in detail in my previous book **'DIY Income'**.

Other options could include a couple more investments from Vanguard :

The first is their **FTSE UK Equity Income fund (Inc)** - the idea is simple, to give investors access to a broad range of approx. 130 dividend-paying securities from across the FTSE 350, while reducing the risk of being overly invested in a small number of high-paying shares or particular industry sectors by limiting the percentage of the index invested in any one company or industry. At the time of writing, the yield is around 4.8% p.a.

The second is their **FTSE All World High Dividend ETF** (VHYL) - the index consists of over 1000 higher yielding large and mid-cap companies listed all around the world. The distribution of income is made quarterly.

The current average yield (2019) is around 3.5% which would produce an annual income of £350 for every £10,000 in the pot.

Finally, there is a managed **Global Equity Income fund** with slightly higher annual charges of 0.60% and a yield of 3.1%.

Selling Units

Some investors will prefer to draw down just the natural yield from their higher yielding investments. This is what I have done with my pension SIPP over the past few years. However, it seems to me this would involve higher level of complexity which may be undesirable or unnecessary by those who are looking to keep things as simple as possible.

The alternative could therefore be to continue with the really simple LifeStrategy fund (or Target Retirement fund) and just siphon off the 'growth' of the fund by selling a small percentage of units on a regular basis. Even though no further contributions are paid into the fund, it will still be growing each year by an average of around 4% or 5% (after inflation and depending on the level of equity) - this is broadly in line with global returns on equities and bonds over the past 20 years. As we have seen above, the average return for the LS40 fund for example since launch in June 2011 has been around 6.5% p.a.

Taking into account fund and platform combined charges of, say 0.4% - 0.5%, it should be possible to sell, say 3% to 4% of your units each year without depleting your pot because the units sold will be replaced by the income and capital growth generated within the fund over the coming year.

Bear in mind that the figure of **6.5% is an AVERAGE** - longer term returns could be lower than this figure and the cautious investor will probably use a lower average of, say, 5%. Also the markets never go up in a straight line so investors will need to prepare for returns to be negative in some years, as in 2018 so it may be prudent to have some form of cash 'buffer' with 2 to 3 yrs reserves if you are mainly depending on investment returns for monthly living expenses.

It may be useful to play around with one of the online tools - one I often make use of is a drawdown calculator provided by Hargreaves Lansdown which can help to decide what level of income would be sustainable over various periods of time. www.hl.co.uk/pensions/drawdown/calculator

You are, of course, free to take whatever amount you want from your investment pot - after all its your money. However, studies have shown that over long periods of over 10 years, taking more than 3.5% - 4.0% out per year will run a higher risk of depleting the pot too quickly.

I have covered this in a little more detail on my blog in relation to SIPP drawdown (pensions) http://diyinvestoruk.blogspot.co.uk/2016/08/a-look-at-sustainable-drawdown.html

(For those interested in doing further research enter 'safe withdrawal rate' into Google).

Tip Set a fixed date each year for your sale of units, transfer the proceeds to an easy access savings account and withdraw over the coming 12 months as required until the next date comes round for the sale of more units.

Scenario 2

Barbara is 62 yrs old and recently retired after 25 yrs working in the NHS. She will receive her state pension in 2023. She owns her house outright. She has been a saver for many years and has £40,000 in various building society accounts. She has been a little disappointed at the low interest rates in recent years. The average is just 1.25% at present giving an annual interest of just £500 per year.

She will take £30,000, half of her tax free lump sum from her pension and has decided to invest this - she would like the option of a little better return than her cash deposits. At the same time, she is fairly cautious by nature and her first instinct is for the capital to be preserved.

She likes the idea of the simplicity of the LS funds and, having looked at the offerings, she feels she would be most comfortable with the lower volatility and lower risk option of a larger percentage in bonds. She therefore opts for the LS40(acc) fund.

Having looked at the Monevator comparison table, she thinks an account with Halifax would be suitable. They will charge £12.50 for a one-off purchase of the investment fund and then an annual flat rate platform fee of £12.50 p.a. She understands that she cannot put the whole amount in an ISA in one tax year as the limit is £20,000 (2019/20) - she therefore opens an ISA and invests £15,000 into the LS40 and will invest the remainder in the next tax year.

She hopes the investment will grow by around £1,200p.a after inflation. When all the funds are invested, she will sell off units to the value of £1,000 p.a. in the first two years - if all goes well, she will increase this to £1,200 p.a. thereafter.

She makes a note to check on the performance of her investment in 12 months time.

12. To Conclude

In this short guide, I have attempted to demonstrate a simple method which I hope most people with average intelligence and a desire to learn, could make sense of without any prior knowledge of stocks and shares.

The aim has been to keep everything as simple as possible which is why I think the one-stop, no frills Vanguard funds with their broad mix of investments and low costs offer an ideal vehicle and therefore worthy of serious consideration by the would-be first time investor.

I make use of a range of Vanguard funds for my personal portfolio - readers can look up the latest by visiting my blog. Furthermore, I have dedicated this book to my grandchildren and I have invested a modest amount for each of them in the LS80 fund with the hope it will grow over the next 20 years or so into a reasonable nest-egg. My aim is to add to the fund over time... I hope they will not be disappointed!

Although this is designed as a simple strategy making use of just one passive index fund, please don't get the wrong impression by thinking a more sophisticated approach using 'absolute' this and 'hedged total return' that will give a better outcome. Over the longer periods, the LifeStrategy index funds will hold their own with other more complex options devised by the professional experts. Indeed, many highly qualified independent financial advisers will recommend these LifeStrategy funds to their clients. Of course these clients will pay a lot of money for this advice and that's money which can be saved by the DIY investor.

Once the strategy has been executed, it should run on auto - you are free to get on with your busy life. Naturally you will want to check how your investments are doing - I would suggest not too frequently - maybe once per year should suffice and also make adjustments to your monthly contributions if you are in the accumulation phase as your income or other circumstances permit.

Patience

Once you have the basic plan in operation, sometimes the hardest thing to do is **NOTHING**. For me and I am sure other small investors, there is always the latest bit of investing snippet to be analysed, the portfolio to be adjusted or tinkered with, a tweak to the plan here or there…

In this short guide, I am trying to set out a few basic rules - this is all well and good, however whilst setting out with good intentions to do the right thing might sound fairly straight forward - human behaviour often gets in the way and investors miss out on achieving a decent return.

Sometimes there is a good reason to make a portfolio change but in my experience, 9 times out of 10 it will be better to do nothing. Successful long term investing is developing a habit of saying 'no' over and over and doing nothing at times when doing 'something' could be a big mistake.

Just being aware that you may be the sort of person who has a tendency to over analyse or tinker may be sufficient to avoid some of the pitfalls. The beauty of a simple one-stop plan is there are not too many decisions to make. Stick to the plan, avoid all the 'noise' in the media and internet forums, keep it simple and most of all - **be patient**.

Warren Buffett's partner, Charlie Munger suggests that even if you are only a slightly above average investor but spend less than you earn, over a lifetime, you will become wealthy - if you are patient. Investing could be described as a process whereby you accept a modest lifestyle today in exchange for a better lifestyle tomorrow.

Many people cannot get to grips with financial affairs because they find it confusing and/or overwhelming - alternatively, they say they don't have much interest as they find it boring. One way to counter these attitudes is to take a little time to learn a little more about investing and then put that education to good use.

Legendary USA investor Benjamin Graham once said *"To achieve satisfactory investment results is easier than most people realize; to achieve superior results is harder than it looks."*

If the reader has reached the end of this short guide, that is an achievement in itself! The aim is not to become an expert in the field of investing and risk management - merely to understand your limitations and, hopefully, implement a simple strategy that will provide a good enough return.

You are probably not going to be the next Warren Buffett or Nick Train but your returns from adopting a low cost passive strategy will likely be better than most investors pursuing a more complex, expensive or active strategy. Also, be aware that the process of investing is not a race and its not a competition - if you are new to investing it will be unfamiliar territory so take it slow and steady, dip a toe in the water and see how it feels. If you have a lump sum to invest, there is no need to commit all on day one. For example, invest say 10% in year 1 and see how it goes - if you feel comfortable with the process, gradually increase the amount invested to your desired allocation.

Whilst I have attempted to outline a simple approach to investing which I hope many ordinary people could embrace, I also accept that it is by no means suitable for everyone as I hope I have made clear earlier in the book. If some people have reached this point and have come to the conclusion that the approach of DIY passive investing is not for them, that is absolutely fine. **It is not the aim of this book to persuade anyone to invest on the stock market** - merely to provide information, options and the (dubious) benefit of my personal experience of what works for me as a small private investor.

Therefore let me just end with the traditional few words of caution. I am not a financial adviser and nothing in this book should be construed as advice. If the reader is in any doubt as to whether an investment strategy outlined above is suitable for their personal circumstances, they should consult a suitably qualified professional adviser.

Thanks for reading and good luck!

To sum up :

* avoid debt - try to save more

* evaluate honestly your attitude to risk and market volatility

* over the long term, equities have performed better than cash or bonds

* be prepared for market volatility with equities

* look to invest for the long term - at least 10 years

* be patient - stay the course

* diversify

* over time, most managed funds fail to beat their benchmark index

* keep costs to a minimum

* finally - KEEP IT SIMPLE!

Copyright © 2019 John Edwards

Some useful websites

Also my blog
www.diyinvestoruk.blogspot.co.uk
(includes links to other blogs in side bar)

Online Stocks & Shares Brokers
www.h-l.co.uk
www.youinvest.co.uk
www.charles-stanley-direct.co.uk
www.halifax.co.uk/sharedealing/
www.iwebsharedealing.co.uk
 www.vanguardinvestor.co.uk/

Fund/ETF Providers
www.vanguard.co.uk/uk/portal/home.jsp
www.ishares.com/uk/individual/en/index.page
www.blackrock.com/uk/home
www.landginvestments.com/funds/multi-index/
www.spdrseurope.com/index.seam

Research
www.digitallook.com
www.trustnet.com/passive-funds/
www.morningstar.co.uk
www.monevator.com
www.theaic.co.uk (investment trusts)

Community
www.moneysavingexpert.com

Other
www.citywire.co.uk
www.thisismoney.co.uk

My other books -

"DIY Introduction to Personal Finance"
"DIY Pensions" and
"DIY Income"

Further Reading

'Smarter Investing' by Tim Hale
'Investing Demystified' by Lars Kroijer
'Little Book of Common Sense Investing' by Jack Bogle

Printed in Great Britain
by Amazon